"I Didn't Know That"

or
(Why We Say The Things We Say)

Volume II

Word and Phrase Origins
Compiled and Edited by Karlen Evins

Published by:
K. Rose Publishing
P.O. Box 150263
Nashville, TN 37215
615-665-2480

First Edition
Printed in the United States
ISBN 0-9635474-1-0

Thanks To The Supporting Cast:

To My Best Friend Teddy,
> For keeping my career on line
> and my life in perspective,
> in spite of all the distractions.

To Andy,
> For sharing your knowledge of the business,
> and your terrific legal mind!

To Uncle Tom,
> For handling business things and numbers-things,
> and jumping right in there when it got over my head!

To Tim,
> For having the patience of Job in setting,
> (and setting...and setting...) this text!

To Angela,
> For your angelic spirit and loving support.

To Dad,
> For supporting the concept,
> for supporting the business,
> for supporting me!

And to Bill,
> For believing in me,
> and loving me through it all!

For my Papaw

Introduction...

Among my favorite childhood memories are visits made to my Granny and Papaw's house in the mountains of East Tennessee. Of all the things I recall from those visits, perhaps my favorite memory has to do with a story my Papaw told me about an Indian named "Falling Rock."

This particular story had to do with a little Indian boy (just my age), named Falling Rock, who wandered away from his family and got lost in the mountains. For days his parents searched for him, but Falling Rock was never to be found. While the story was richly embellished, the conclusion was, that after months and months and years and years of searching, his parents never gave up hope, and eventually resorted to posting signs along the highways that read, "Lookout for Falling Rock!"

Now whether the story was legendary, or whether Papaw created it just for me, really didn't matter. All I know is that for years I would rush in to visit my Papaw, telling him that *I* had seen the signs for Falling Rock and that it must mean his parents were still searching! As I would prepare to leave after each visit with my grandparents, Papaw would dry my sad little eyes by telling me once again, the story of Falling Rock. With each telling, he prepared me for my long ride home by asking me to watch for those signs that read, "Lookout for Falling Rock!"

I'll always cherish those storytimes with Papaw. As a child I begged to hear about Falling Rock with each visit, as no one could tell the story like he did. As an adult, I hastened to record the story in writing, in order to save it for times when Papaw was no longer here to tell it.

In this day of ten-second sound bites and 30-minute newscasts, my biggest concern is that we, as a society, might lose sight of the stories and tellings that comprise our history. In this day of daytimer meetings and faxed communications, who will tell our children the meanings in our expressions, our customs...our lives?

This book is but a small dedication to those who would keep those stories alive. And to Papaw, for being the kind of grandpa every child should have.

From the French word "amator," our word *amateur* translates to mean "a lover." Today the word connotes one lacking the experience to be called a professional, but the original meaning dealt more with motive rather than ranking. The first *amateur* engaged in a pastime for the LOVE of that pastime, as opposed to taking on

the task for money. For the artist or the athlete today who truly loves the profession he's chosen, perhaps a "professional" *amateur* label would best apply.

The word we use today to describe one's fervent desire to get somewhere, came to us from the Latin word "ambitio," which literally translates: "go getter." The first go-getters were ancient Romans...more

specifically, Roman politicians, who were going to get votes. Because political recognition was something to be desired (especially if you were a commoner, aspiring for more than just the simple life), the "ambitios" were those who sought fame and power by way of politics to better their own lots in life.

Just the thought of it makes you squirm, doesn't it? Well, that was the idea! *Ants in the pants* was actually an old English folk remedy for "tired blood." In the late-1700s, belief was that if someone slept more than his fair share, or was more lethargic than normal, an antidote was in order. To quicken circulation, one

prescription of the day was to place *ants in the pants* of the patient. Another, believe it or not, called for placing a "bee in one's bonnet!" (Thank goodness for modern medicine, huh?)

Some say it has to do with the apples IN the pies, others will tell you it had to do with the arrangement of apple pies ON the shelf, but the bottom line is that the phrase *apple pie order* dates back to the days of the early

pioneers, when wives of the frontiersmen did their baking at the first of the week. Arranging the apples within the pie, and arranging the pies on the shelves once they were cooked, were both neat and orderly procedures, which gave us our *apple pie order* meaning today.

The first to be *armed to the teeth*, was an ancient Nordic tribe known as the Berserkers, whose teeth were their most deadly weapons! These particular tribesmen were known for filing their teeth into sharp points, and savagely attacking their opponents, who, most often carried more civilized weapons like swords, spears or

clubs. Originally *armed to the teeth*, meant to be barely armed at all, but historically, its meaning of "being on the attack, prepared for any confrontation," carries over today.

Think *backseat driver* and you think of one who complains, or one who thinks he can see better from the rear than from the front of a vehicle. But the original *backseat drivers* weren't complainers. Matter of fact, for

what they were watching, they COULD see better! In days of the early fire engines, there was a job for *backseat drivers*. Someone needed to watch the ladder as engines rushed to the scene. As quick turns and abrupt stops were cause for accidents, a *backseat driver* was as vital a part of the fire team as the fire fighters themselves!

To *balk*...to stop short, to pause before proceeding as though an obstacle were in the way, is, by definition, a word to stop for! The word itself comes from the Old English word "balca," which is a beam. In the days before locks, these beams were placed across doors to keep out enemies and unwanted intruders. Because it stopped

those attempting to enter a beamed door, as well as stalling the one removing the balca from the inside, the meaning of stopping or stalling carries over today.

In the late-1800s with the increasing popularity of baseball, ballparks became the hangout for large events, both sports-related and otherwise. Political candidates often found ballparks the best setting for their

rallies, but because no tickets were sold for these events, news-paper reporters were forced to estimate a *ballpark number* in covering the attendance. When one party would overestimate its side's support, the rival party would in turn do the same, and as a result, *ballpark figures* turned out to be very rough, often inaccurate counts.

No need *beating around the bush*, unless you're a hunter looking for game. As many hunters will tell you, it is sometimes necessary to scare the game into running or flying before one can shoot. *Beating the bushes* was customary hunting procedure long ago. Yet, for one

Beating Around the Bush

who really did not enjoy the sport of killing an animal, *beating around the bush* was a way to scare off game so that nothing was left for the confrontation.

There is an Old English custom whereby married couples, who were willing to swear upon a Bible that they hadn't fought in a year, were rewarded a side of bacon for their feat. Yet whether that custom gave us our current meaning for

(to) Bring Home the Bacon

bringing home the bacon, is doubtful. Most will tell you that *bringing home the bacon*, is American in origin, and that it dates back to the greased pig contests of old county fairs. As the catcher was the keeper, the expression speaks for itself.

The symbols we use today to refer to the status of the stock market, actually began on the London stock market long ago. There, trading notices were posted (literally) on cork bulletin boards by hand. The British brokers of the 18th century called these stock bulletins, "bulls!" and you could find such, plastered on the

Bulls and Bears

board at the end of a heavy trading day. Obviously, when trading was less than busy, the bulletin board was "bare," and the contrast of the two is how we came to call them *bulls and bears* today!

Like so many colorful expressions, chewing the fat originated on the high seas. Think back to the early days of sailing, PRE-refrigeration, when the only foods carried on long trips were those requiring NO refrig-

eration. One such item was salt pork. As no part of the meat went to waste (including the skin), *chewing the fat* was common fare between meals and sometimes as meal substitutes. It was later in the 1870s that chewing the fat became the catch phrase for idle chatter that originally went along with the REAL chewing that took place aboard ships of old.

Inventor of the *cocktail* was one Antoine Amedee Peychaud, a druggist from the West Indies who came to New Orleans in the late-1700s. Famous for the invention of Peychaud's Bitters, Antoine once mixed a special drink of bitters and brandy in an egg cup known as a "coquetier," (pronounced "kok-tyay"). So popular became the drink that soon, cafés and bars in New Orleans picked up on the concoction; thus, the first "cocktails" were born.

The first *cold shoulder* referred to a cold shoulder of meat, given to a sojourner who might stop along the course of his travels to ask for food. As mutton was the common course of old English farmhouses, it was

customary for a traveler to be given a *cold shoulder* and be sent along his way. A warm meal would have indicated an invitation to stick around a bit longer, but a *cold shoulder* was a sign that the traveler would be fed, but should expect no more.

It was long ago that Eric, King of Sweden, hit upon a certain village with a handful of his best soldiers to overtake the area. As the townspeople watched, they soon determined that Eric's soldiers were neither numerous nor skilled, so the threat of the siege soon diminished. In mockery, the locals hung a goose in the middle of

Cooking One's Goose

town for target practice for the King's men. As the story goes, King Eric became so angry that he burned the entire village, cooking goose and all! The phrase was popularized by a London ballad some years later.

Those insincere tears we've come to know as *crocodile tears* are quite literal in origin. For you see, a crocodile does indeed cry over its meal as it eats. But the crying has nothing to do with the croc's sense of the situation.

Instead, as a crocodile eats, his food is pressed to the top of his mouth, causing pressure a-gainst the glands known as the lachrymals. These secrete a tear-like substance that flow from the eyes. From this biological activity of the reptile, we today draw our meaning for *crocodile tears*.

How many of us remember from our Sunday School days that God gave the ark dimensions to Noah in *cubits* rather than feet? Well if you do, you probably remember being told that a *cubit* was about 18 inches, but how do we know? Truth is, the word cubit comes from the Latin word "cubitus," meaning "a bend." At the

Cubit

time, the distance between the bend of the arm (i.e. elbow), and the second finger was your basic *cubit*. Obviously the size varied between individuals, but most measured somewhere between 18 and 22 inches.

The first *dead beats* were technically "debt beaters." These were people who avoided their creditors by leaving their debts behind. In the early days of this country, there were

two ways to shirk your financial obligations: (1) by declaring bankruptcy or (2) by actually moving out of the colony where the debt was incurred. Those choosing the latter, were known as "debt beaters," which later was shortened and mispronounced, as *deadbeats!*

It was the French who gave us both the word and the custom of *dessert*. By definition, their word "desservir" meant "to clear the table," which originally consisted of clearing both dishes and tablecloth to make way for the final presentation. Most often that final course was a pastry or ice cream, but in all cases it was something  sweet to end the meal with. It was believed then that the sugar in the *dessert* was necessary to give a rush of energy in order to digest all the foods consumed in the meal.

Yes, there truly was an original *dingbat!* And it was a very important part of vaudeville. Where sticks were often used for sound effects from the vaudeville stage (see slapstick), bells were also used at the punchline of a joke.

This same stick was used for both batting the bells that marked the comic's buffoonery, and for sounding the final curtain call from the vaudeville show. From this association, the term *dingbat* soon became the word to comically describe one whose mental capacity was in question.

The history of *Donnybrook* goes back to the early 13th century. Donnybrook, Ireland, a small village just west of Dublin, was notorious for its fair, held annually around the end of August. The Donnybrook Fair was quite an event for the area, and as a result, much drinking and carousing was done. As over-crowded and

quick-tempered Irishmen were quick to pack a punch, the event soon became notorious for its fighting frenzies. Originally the fair lasted two weeks, later this was shortened to one. Later yet (mid-1800s), the fair was discontinued all together, due to its riots.

Those who work with wool know that if you attempt to dye an item after it is already spun into cloth, the odds of having an even, colorfast result are slim to none. The proper way to dye wool is to color the raw material

Dyed in the Wool

before it is ever woven. By the same token, one said to be *dyed in the wool* is a person who is thoroughly indoctrinated with a belief, who believes in his cause through and through, and who leaves no gaps, no holes, no openings for any change in his opinion.

It was the early American Indian who was first credited with keeping an *ear to the ground*. Perhaps you were told, (as the first frontiersmen believed) that this was done in order to listen for horses' hooves as cowboys approached. However, native American Indians will tell you the custom had to do with a certain spiritual

Ear to
the
Ground

belief. As they felt the land was sacred, most Indians held the view that listening to Mother Earth would protect them. To do this, they placed their *ears to the ground* in order to hear her heartbeat, and to be one with her nature.

As the War of 1812 was coming to a close, story has it that an American soldier crossed British lines while hunting for game. Finding nothing better, the American shot a crow, but being overheard by a British officer, the

Eat Crow

soldier was forced to eat the crow as punishment for being on British soil. As the story goes, halfway through the act, the American turned on the British soldier, making HIM eat the remaining crow. As a result, *eating crow* came to mean having to do something that one simply did not want or mean to do.

Think of the most *eccentric* person you know, and I bet you're thinking "strange!" By definition, the *eccentric* personality is one that falls "outside the normal pattern of behavior." But more specifically, the word *eccentric* is a geometric one. Derived from the Greek word "ekkentros" ("ex" meaning "out of"; "kentron" meaning

"center"), the precise translation of *eccentric* is "off centered" or just a little out of balance. Makes perfectly good sense that the *eccentric* personality is one that is just a little off the mark!

By definition, going to *extremes* means going way out of range, or going out of bounds. The original *extremes* were places in the early Middle Ages. From the Latin word "extremus," the *extremes* were areas of land set just beyond the boundries of town, designated solely for the socially outcast. As this area was situated as far from the center of town as was possible, *extremes* became synonymous with living way out of bounds due to one's behavior being way out of line.

In the Middle Ages, it was once customary for men to wear cloaks with hoods indicating their professions. Doctors were known by one style of hood, clergymen another, artists and musicians yet another. In associating hood-style with profession, most anyone could tell at a glance what business a man was in. Unfortunately, the

downside to this concept came when one attempted to pass himself off as professional in a field for which he had no background. In such a case, the *false hood* worn gave meaning to the deception attempted.

It was the early flintlock musket that required a pan for the priming powder to spark the flint. Often when one pulled the trigger of a musket, nothing happened,

Flash in the Pan

because the hammer that struck the flint did not generate a spark strong enough to ignite the powder. To watch the spark fizzle in the shallow pan holding the powder, gave us our image of a *flash in the pan*. To this day we hold its meaning to be something that dazzles, but doesn't get the job done!

We think of *fly-by-nights* as those shady, less-than-honorable businesses or business people that are here one day, then gone the next. But the first reference to a *fly-by-night* was a superstitious one that described, quite literally, a witch! Because she flew by broom at night, the witch was seen as one, evil in nature, and up

Fly-By-Night

to no good. (In England, however, the *fly-by-night* had a totally different origin, so be careful if you use this phrase overseas! There, *fly-by-nights* were once prostitutes, who did their business in the darkness of night, and flew away by the light of day.)

The first thing to lose its head, and *fly off the handle* was the common ax, and it was the early pioneers who gave us this phrase. The earliest axes were made by hand, with the blade hammered out by blacksmiths or steel workers. Handles were

Fly Off the Handle

workers. Handles were whittled by frontiersmen, and as a result, the fit wasn't always the best. At times, it was com-mon to see an ax head fly right off the handle, mid-chop, often hurting nearby woodsmen. This unexpected trouble soon became synonymous with anger and the loss of control. The image, as a figure of speech, just stayed with us through time.

The first sponging off of others, or *freeloading*, as the word is defined, took place in the pubs of merry old England. Unofficial rules once had it that when 5 or 6 friends got together to drink, each would pay for a round, until all had contributed to the evening. One who would accept drinks and then leave the pub

before his turn to pay, basically got loaded for free, hence the term *freeloader*. (Interesting to note that in Northern England, the one who left early was said to be "shy his pint of beer," and was thus, called a *pint-shyer*, as opposed to a *freeloader*.)

To fudge, or to hedge, is basically to avoid an honest answer, which is precisely what the first fudgers did! It wasn't long after the first automobiles came out that some salesmen attempted to pitch their shabbier USED cars

as better than they really were. To keep the knocks and pings from sounding, scheisters were known to put gum in the joints (i.e. *gumming up the engine*), or they put putty between the parts. When fudge was introduced, it was the perfect disguise. Not only was it sludge-colored, but it melted away after the conned customer drove his new purchase off the lot!

A word we take for granted, but one with an interesting origin all the same, the *garden,* as it was originally spelled in old English, was a most sacred place. Because they contained the substance of life, gardens, in medieval times, were the responsibility of monks; as a result, you could find one near every abbey and

monastery. Before long, the monks devised walls and fences to protect their plots, and these areas were soon referred to as the "guarded" lands. Later translated, "garden," the word soon came to stand for any land set aside for growing, guarded with walls or not.

While several accounts exist for the origin of *goblin,* perhaps the most popular dates back to the early-1400s. At that time a beautiful bright red fabric came out of Paris, France, created by Gilles and Jehan Gobelin. So

stunning was this cloth that the superstitious and jealous locals of the day started rumors suggesting that the brothers MUST have sold their souls to the devil in exchange for the color. As a result, the "Gobelins" were ostracized, and their names were made synonymous with the word we now associate with evil or mischief.

Also known as *goose flesh*, *goose pimples* are those bumps you get when your skin takes a chill! For obvious reasons, *goose pimples* were named for their similarity to the skin of a plucked goose! Long ago, goose feathers were used for a miriad of things; thus, some birds were plucked up to five times a year. From these pluckings,

farmers soon noticed the reaction of *goose flesh* to the cold, as the birds' skin contracted to pull up what would have been feathers. This *goose flesh* was soon associated with the same bumpy-skin effect that cold or certain emotions had on humans.

This one we borrowed from the Great Depression, when diners and cafeterias found it customary to save every scrap of food. Any and all excess was salvaged, and restaurant owners soon started setting aside their

leftovers for beggars and the homeless. It became customary for these leftover scraps to be set at the end of the

lunch counter, bagged and ready to go, for anyone who might be in need. Thus, the expression *up for grabs* became the catch phrase for those morsels of food, set UP on the counter for the needy to GRAB.

If you don't know which Scott we're referring to here, you should, so take note! *Great Scott* refers to one Winfred Scott, commander of the Mexican War and the Whig party's nomination for president in the election of 1852. Known for being rather struck on himself, Scott's campaign was marked with pride and arrogance, yet he

campaigned with great fervency. His opposition referred to him as, "Great Scott!" in making fun of his pomposity, and as a result, we use the phrase pretentiously today. (Incidentally, Great Scott was defeated by Franklin Pierce. It just goes to show...)

While the *guinea pig* has long been associated with laboratory experimentation, the connotation of a used person is much more colorful. Early stock companies in England often acquired noblemen to sign as

their directors for the for sake of credibility. The only legal obligation was that the figurehead attend an annual meeting (usually a luncheon or dinner), where he was paid a director's fee of one guinea (approximately 21 shillings). The pun referred to the token fee, and the free meal received for allowing the company to use his name.

There WAS an actual ring that gave us the image of politicians tossing their *hats in the ring* in announcing their desire to run for public office. That ring was in Vienna, Austria and was known as "The Ringstrasse" or Ring Street. Those seeking public office were known to go to this "boulevard peripherique," not only to

address the crowds about their candidacy, but to solicit support (hat in hand) for campaign contributions. The concept and phrase made it to America by way of our Austrian immigrants.

It's easy enough to conjure up the image of a machine with a screw loose, but which machine originally gave us the phrase? Well, it was the cotton gin, the advent of which caused cotton mills to multiply at an

To Have a Screw Loose

unbelievable rate in the 1700s. So frequent were the breakdowns of the earliest machines, that loose screws were nearly always blamed for the problem. As a result, the phrase was adapted by most everyone who needed to blame something or someone for just about anything. By the early 1800s, *having a screw loose* became the catch phrase for something gone amiss.

Cartoonist Billy DeBeck is credited with coining this phrase in the late-1940s, but the origin traces even further. It is believed that DeBeck took the name from a dance made popular in the 1920s. Yet looking further still, the words "hiba jiba" were first noted by European missionaries visiting the African Congos. The natives

there referred to "hiba-jiba" in describing one "out of his skin." It was believed that evil spirits provoked "hiba-jibas" as they attempted to leave a person. That same agitated, jittery feeling is basically the same meaning we attach to *heebie jeebies* today.

Heydays of old were literally feast days, and were a product of the feudal system. In medieval times, a serf who tended to his lord's manor was entitled to both military protection, and a portion of the harvest. In

addition to the produce that a serf might take for his family, he was given one *hay day* each year to store up hay for his livestock. This "payment day" was usually set aside at the end of each harvest (somewhere in mid-October) and was followed by great celebration and feasting, which gives us our association with the word today.

The country *hick* is quite American in origin, dating back to the early American schoolrooms. As the need for formal education increased, so did theories on how best to instruct. Controversial were the precepts of corporal punishment, and many of the more progressive thinkers challenged its value. Those country

folk who held to the belief of "spare the rod and spoil the child," were said to be from "hickory towns," those towns whose schools still utilized hickory sticks in disciplining their school children. From that, we condensed and created our word *hick* today.

Taken from the Old English, *hobnob* literally translates: "have and have not," or "to give and take." In taverns of old, that's exactly what transpired! Famous for socializing in their local pubs, the English were quick to

offer a toast on behalf of their closest friends. As one had to give, and another receive, hob- nobbing was quite the social event of the day. And as drinks were bought in rounds (see *freeloader*), the word *hobnob* had as much to do with the giving and taking of information as it did with the giving and taking of ale!

The public outcry we now refer to as *hue and cry* was, in its early day, a law-enforcement tactic. Long ago, when one was robbed, he was said to yell, "with hue and with cry" or "with horn and with voice." At this, the townspeople were to drop what they were doing and go in search of the criminal. The word "hue" we took

from the French, "huer," which meant "to shout." Add a "cry" to whatever evil befell you, and the alarm was triggered for the public to go after the offender. Today, the phrase is synonymous with ANY loud disturbance, independent of criminal offense.

The phrase, *in a pickle* came to us from the Dutch, and does refer to the salt solution used some four centuries ago in preserving pickles. Yet, as pickle barrels were transported to this country, their juice was soon

In a
Pretty
Pickle

discovered to have other preserving qualities as well. Stored in barrels, in the hulls of large boats, this same pickled water was also found to be quite useful in preserving the occasional human who happened to die while making the trip across the seas. For one to be *in a pickle* meant he was in a poor state, indeed!

The oldest reference to *in the bag* is said to have come from hunting lingo, with the "bag" being that used to bag game. But a more local and colorful explanation also exists. It has to do with cock fighting, that illegal competition between gamecocks (traditionally fitted with spurs), that fight until the death of one

of the contestants. As prize gamecocks were usually transported in cloth bags, "cocky" owners have been credited with the phrase as they boasted their victory was *in the bag* prior to a fight ever taking place.

In the groove is actually one of our more recent expressions, and we're happy to claim it as purely American in origin. A product of the swing era, *in the groove* has to do with the advent of the phonograph, more

specifically, the needle and the record. If you were into counting grooves, you would find that there is but one, long continuous groove per record. But only in keeping the phonograph needle *in the groove* can you be assured of keeping the music flowing smoothly.

To be *in the hole*, as it refers to being in debt, originated in the gambling houses of old. Poker was the preferred game of the mid-1800s, and it was during poker's popularity, that gambling house owners prospered. As a certain percentage of each game went to the house, cash was stuffed in a slot or hole in the center of each table.

In the Hole

The money was secured in a box underneath. Those losers who wound up their nights with more money *in the hole* than in their pockets were said to BE *in the hole*. The association of being without cash, has remained ever since.

Granted, a lamb IS known to shake its tail twice as fast as most any other animal, but the expression, *in two shakes of a lamb's tail*, seems to be an extension of a more popular

In Two
Shakes of
a Lamb's
Tail

British phrase, *in two shakes*. Both refer to something done in an instantaneous amount of time: yet, one was coined in the mid-1800s and refers to a small sheep, while the other dates back much further, and has to do with the quick shaking of a dice box, just before those dice are rolled.

Historically speaking, punishment for crime has come in a variety of forms, but until most recently, one thing shared by most societies was public display. From the stockades to the guillotines, public punishments were events for all to see, serving as both a deterrent and a societal function. At one time, it was common practice to  imprison thieves and robbers in large iron cages, hung slightly above ground level for all to see. It was from this particular punishment that the word *jailbird* was coined, playing off the obvious resemblance of the criminal to a bird in a cage.

Believe it or not, *in a jam* has a history in the hunting arena, and the phrase is said to date back to the early-1800s. Appalachian frontiersmen were said to have discovered that homemade jam and fruit preserves were

quite an attraction to animals such as raccoons, skunks and even bears! Before long, *jam* became the bait for trappings. When a scavenger, lured by the smell of the fruits and seasonings, was caught, *in a jam,* nearby hunters would shoot away! The phrase quickly spread throughout the east, to describe any sticky or difficult situation.

As you probably know, these rugged, all-terrain vehicles were originally built for the United States Army, and were especially useful in times of war. When the first quarter-ton reconnaissance cars were delivered, the letters "G.P." were painted on their doors. Now the "G.P." was short for "General Purpose,"  which was precisely the function of these sturdy, land-climbing jewels! The word "jeep" was simply a shorter, more familiar version of "G.P," as it was read on the doors of the vehicles.

Several stories exist for the word *josh*. One has it that the Scottish word, "joss," meaning to push against or jostle, may have started it all. Another theory has it that the word is early American and is a combination of joke

and bosh (the latter meaning "foolish talk"). But whatever its origin, the popularity of *josh* came about when American humorist and writer Josh Billings made it famous in the mid-1800s. Known for his misspelled words, his humorous grammar and his literary puns, Josh's name became synonymous with the joking style in which he wrote.

A fairly recent addition to our language, the first mention of *Jumbo* was in reference to an elephant, purchased by P.T. Barnum in 1881. Jumbo was captured in West Africa in 1869 and was the largest elephant known to man at the time. Weighing in at six-and-a-half tons, *Jumbo* was a favorite at the London Zoological Society,

which is where P.T. found him. Barnum was reported to have paid $30,000 for *Jumbo*, and was said to have re-cooped his investment ten-fold within 6 weeks. Thanks to Jumbo's size and P.T.'s marketing, *Jumbo* became THE word for the largest thing going!

May we never forget! *Keeping Up With the Joneses* was a comic strip, made popular in the early-1900s. The creation of cartoonist Arthur ("Pop") Momand ran in American newspapers for over 28 years. Having

struggled himself to keep up with others in classes above his own, Momand was said to have created the cartoon out of his own experience before moving out of an upscale neighborhood with his wife. Interestingly enough, Momand originally considered *Keeping Up With the Smiths* as the name for his cartoon, but settled on Joneses, thinking it sounded better.

Short for "kidding gloves," the first kid gloves were designed for the very wealthy in 14th century England. Because workers of the day needed work gloves to protect their hands, they found the fingerless, non-practical gloves to be a joke, and thus referred to them as *fake-* or *kidding- gloves.* The phrase, *to treat someone with kid*

gloves was a further mockery of the upper class, as by all means, they would never have a need for gloves other than to show their social status. As a result, we today use the phrase to connote treating someone pretentiously special.

Much like the word sounds, *kindergarten* was a term meaning "children's garden." It was coined by the German instructor Friedrich Froebel, who believed that the mind of the child should be given the respect

and attention one would give a garden. It was Froebel who came up with the concept of a school for the very young, to allow children the opportunity to play, to construct and to exercise their minds, cultivating natural abilities and aptitudes in the confines of a schoolroom setting.

From the Dutch, the word "boedel" means "effects," or those things that a person owns. Thieves adapted the word, calling whatever they stole the "boodle." Pirates used the same base of reference in referring to the "booty" they took from ships they attacked. As burglars tools were carried

Kit and Caboodle

in their "kits," a clean sweep of a house was often referred to as getting away with "the kit and the boodle." It is from this combination, that our phrase *kit and caboodle* was coined.

To know a person inside and out, or *to know him like a book*, goes back to the days when there were very FEW books. Matter of fact, the Bible would be one good example of just how the phrase came into being. Before printing presses made household items out of Bibles (and later, other books), people had to memorize scriptures and stories in order to pass the information along. Monks of old were perhaps the first to know something from cover to cover, as one would know a book. The expression speaks for itself.

To Know
(Him/Her)
Like a Book

The Chinese word "k'o t'ou" (pronounced "KO' tow"), literally translates, "knock your head," which is precisely what the commoners were to do as they bowed before their leaders. Ancient Chinese custom was for inferiors to bow head to floor as anyone in authority within the Chinese Empire walked by. As a result, foreigners who

witnessed the act interpreted *kowtowing* to be a form of brown-nosing. The word is believed to have been brought over by early missionaries who couldn't comprehend the subservient behavior.

Perhaps *lady* today means a female of refined habits and gentle manners, but the original *lady* was hardly so stylish! From the Middle English word, "ladfi," the first *lady* was nothing more than a "kneader of bread!"

Before you jest, keep in mind that the lord of the manner was likewise named for being the "keeper of the bread." Together the two maintained their household. Seeing how lords and ladies were those who HAD households to maintain in the first place (as opposed to being mere workers for another) the first *lady* did hold some power, through the food she produced.

The original *lame duck* was a member of the British Stock Exchange who couldn't meet his liabilities on settlement date, and thus, flew off without settling his account. From that we applied the term to our own political candidates, who, by way of losing an election, can't return to the flock, even though their own party has  been retained. Much as it would be for a wounded bird that could no longer fly, the *lame duck* candidate becomes the responsibility of the new administration, and is taken care of, often given some appointment to an office that does not require election.

From the Old English word "loewed," this word was originally a label for the *lay* person, or one not in the clergy. As that most often meant one who was ignorant, the word was used to describe those who were

unlearned...hence, common. From this, the definition was carried down to mean base, and later took on the connotation of vulgar in both language and behavior. All from a simple attempt to separate the commoners from the more righteous clergy, the word *lewd* today now means sexually unchaste and all but evil.

The *lion's share,* meaning all, or nearly all, comes from an Aesop fable about a lion, a fox and an ass that went hunting. Upon returning with their kill, the lion asked the ass to divide their spoils, allotting each his share. The ass divided each share equally and allowed his partners to pick their own. At this, the lion roared and  killed the ass, taking that part with his. The lion then asked the fox to divide the remaining goods, upon which the fox took only a small portion. When asked how he learned his math so well, the fox's reply was, "by noting what happened to the ass!"

In castles of old, *loopholes* were a common architectural structure built into the walls themselves, as form of security for times of war. These small openings, spaced every few feet apart, were designed for both

observation, as well as for firing small weapons like arrows. While the holes were small and narrow, if need be, they could serve as a rough means of escape should the castle be taken under attack. It is from this context that our current definition of a *loophole,* as a way out of a problem at hand, came into being.

While Lewis Carroll may have given animation to the expression *Mad As A March Hare* through his Alice In Wonderland character, the reason behind the phrase is more natural than that in origin. It has to do with the breeding season for certain types of hares... more specifically, the buck hare. The buck hare, has

been long noted for the crazy antics he takes on with the change of seasons. For instance, with the onset of spring breeding time, the buck hare frolics in ways that appear quite insane to one observing his habits, and from this, the expression was borne.

In days of old, when cooking was done over an open fire, it wasn't uncommon to find a variety of items all cooking in one pot. Often, scraps of meat were tossed in the mix (as is the reference for *gone to pot*), and as a result,

Make No
Bones
About It

bones were pretty much inevitable. True, it required a degree of caution as you ate, seeing as you might run across a bone in your stew. Yet, while the more particular guest might complain of the bones in his bowl, those who simply appreciated the meal, making no big deal of the occasional inconvenience, were said to have *made no bones about it*.

While many may hope to make their mark in the world, few perhaps actually do so. Nonetheless, at one point in time, *making one's mark* meant simply, distinguishing one's work from another's. More specifically, it was the practice of smiths and artisans of long ago, to mark their wares with a symbol or logo placed somewhere

on the art piece. Once that mark became generally well-known, the artist was said to have *made his mark* in the world, thus indicating true success.

The word we use today to mean weak, insipid or emotional, came to us from biblical times. The word *maudlin* was the British pronunciation of Magdalene...more specifically, Mary

Magdalene of Jesus's day. As Medieval painters depicted Mary Magdalene with doleful face and swollen eyes from her weeping over the death of her lord, the term *maudlin* soon became synonymous with sadness, melancholy and sentiment as we know it to be used today.

It was in Texas around the mid-1800s that cattle branding was all the rage for those wanting to identify their cattle by way of their own ranch. It was Samuel Maverick, owner of one of the largest ranches around, who decided that in NOT branding his cattle, would they be best identified. Maverick declared that any

cattle found without a brand was his own. As this method would've included all wild and unclaimed beasts as well his own, his attempts failed. But his name soon came to mean anything that hadn't been claimed by a prior group.

That annoying, irritating word *nag* comes from the Scandinavian word "gnaga," which means "to gnaw.' It was during the Middle Ages that rat infestation in Europe was fairly common. That, coupled with squirrels that

often nested in thatched roofs, made for gnawing, annoying sounds throughout the night. It was from this nerve-racking sound that the shortened word *nag* was formed. In comparing one who gnaws at another by way of complaining, to that same annoying sound of rat-gnawing, *nag* has taken on its current meaning today.

The *mud* referred to in this context has to do with Dr. Samuel Mudd, the hapless physician who happened to set the broken leg of John Wilkes Booth, shortly after the assassination of President Abraham Lincoln. Though strictly abiding by his profession's code of ethics, Dr. Mudd was, as a result of his action, sentenced to a life in  prison for helping an assassin. Nonetheless, even in prison, Mudd gained recognition for the tremendous contribution he made in working with patients of the typhoid epidemic.

The word *nepotism*, used to describe favoritism to a relative within a certain job context, was first coined during the reign of Pope Alexander VI. Noted as perhaps the most political pope of all, Alexander is

remembered for filling more positions within the church by way of his own relatives, than any other pope in history. Direct from the Latin word "nepos," *nepotism* originally referred to any descendant, especially a nephew or grandson. Today the word includes any and all family shown favoritism strictly on the basis of kinship.

The Old English word "mare" described a certain kind of evil spirit, imagined to be female, thought to be much like a goblin or monster. The *nightmare* was believed to disturb a person's sleep by sitting on the chest of the sleeper, causing a feeling of suffocation and terror in the night. As a result, the term *night-mare* later became the word for both the

spirit, as well as the feeling produced. Today, we simply use the word to describe any frightening dream or experience that occurs while one is sleeping.

Anyone *not worth his salt,* is worth very little indeed, and by some definitions, not worth the money he earns. In days of old, the Romans were known to give rations of salt and other necessities to their soldiers and

civil servants. These portions fell under the general category of "sal" (in Latin), and when money became the substitute, the word "salarium," (base word for our word salary), was borne. In a reversed context, the English phrase "true to his salt," refers to one faithful to his employer.

The first official *odds and ends* were found in lumber yards, as they were, quite literally, leftover scraps of wood. *Odds* were those pieces of board split irregularly by the sawmill, that were less than even in shape. The *ends* were those end pieces trimmed off boards that were cut to specific lengths. Some dishonest lumberers

were said to have sold these *odds and ends* to unknowing customers, by adding the inches of the pieces in question, and including them in the total footage count upon delivery.

While many theories exist for the origin of this phrase, one of the more predominant ones has to do with the early days of nightclubs, and the colored spotlights focused on the featured performer. As hosts

and emcees were often known to work their material in between acts, some were known to use their less clean versions to the side of center stage (and center spotlight), thereby dodging the spotlight if the audience took offense. By this *off color* performance do some claim the phrase took on its risqué meaning today.

The initials *O.K.* refer to a certain political organization formed in support of presidential candidate Martin Van Buren, when he was running for re-election in 1840. The members supporting Van Buren formed "The Democratic O.K. Club," with the *O.K.* standing for Old Kinderhook, a nick-name given Van Buren  that was taken from his hometown of Kinderhook, located near the Hudson Valley. As *O.K.* became the catch-phrase of the day, its meaning soon came to be known as "alright," and it's since taken on that same association today.

When carpets were first introduced, it was obvious that only the well-to-do could afford to cover their floors. As this meant only the master or mistress of the house would have

carpeted rooms, it was fair to say that the servants only stood on carpets when they were called in for a reprimand or termination. From this practice, dating back to the early-1800s, our current meaning for one *called on the carpet* came into being.

To *ostracize* means to banish or exclude from social interaction, and its origin is most fascinating. We get the word from the Greek word, "ostrakon," which is a tile or a shell. As it was customary for the ancient Greeks to send into exile any person whose power was considered dangerous to the state, "ostrakons" were used  in deciding the matter. The name of the person to be banished was written on a tile, and a vote was taken. Since then, the word for the tile has been substituted for the action associated therewith.

Interestingly enough, *overwhelm* means basically the same as *whelm*, though perhaps the "over" part adds more emphasis. Both mean "completely overcome by something," but it's the *whelm* part that adds

its meaning. From the Middle English word "whelven," the meaning behind *whelm* has to do with a capsized boat, or a vessel turned upside down. From this 13th century word whelm did we create *overwhelm*, as meaning "something completely covered over" (in the original case, "with water").

Whether pronounced "Oh yez" or "Oh yea," the word *oyez*, has nothing to do with our word "yes" at all. *Oyez* comes to us from the Old French word, "oiez," taken from the French verb, "oir." Translated, the word means, "to hear." Used

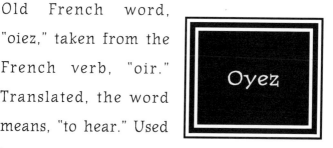

by a court or public crier to gain attention before a proclamation, the words, "oyez, oyez," simply mean, "Listen up!" or "Hear this!"

Any freelance photographer who aggressively pursues a celebrity for the purpose of obtaining that perfect candid shot is said to be a part of the *paparazzi*, but what exactly is a *paparazzi*?

Well, the word is Italian in origin, and literally translated, means "buzzing insects." (Anyone having seen the hoopla surrounding the better known celebs of our time, knows exactly where the word gets its meaning!)

To pay too much for something has long been the meaning behind *paying through the nose,* though it can also mean paying in installments, (which would, in most cases, ALSO mean paying a higher price). The phrase is said to have originated in Sweden back many years ago. At one time, the Swedish government

Paying Through the Nose

charged a nose tax of one penny per person, which was basically nothing more than a head tax. Nonetheless, *paying through the nose* became synonymous for paying too much, (which is not much different from what we feel about paying our taxes today!)

First you must know that peanuts are called such because they grow as peas in a pod. Similarly, the *peanut gallery*, that audience of people, usually seated in the back of a theatre, looks like a bunch of peas in a pod,

Peanut
Gallery

from the performer's perspective on stage. The original peanut gallery referred to the cheap seats, second balcony up, in the theatres of the Gay Nineties. The name was coined not only from the appearance of the crowds, but also from the fact that the commoners in those seats were known to throw peanut shells at any actor or actress they particularly did not like.

In case you don't recall the story, Peeping Tom of Coventry, England, was the man who used a peep-hole to look at Lady Godiva as she rode through town, "...clothed only in chastity." As the story has it, Tom was a tailor, and he was stricken with blindness for disobeying the order given all the townspeople not to look

at the Countess as she made her famous ride. (You might recall that Lady Godiva made her ride after begging her husband, Earl Leofric of Mercia, to take away an oppressive tax on the poor, which he said he would do if she would ride unclothed through town!)

Buying a *pig in a poke* means you've bought something unseen, or that you've been scammed. The word "poke" in this case refers to a small sack or bag. From the French expression, "Acheter un chat en poche," (or

Pig in a Poke

"buying a cat in a poke,") the reference made is to an old trick of substituting a cat for a baby pig. When one, thinking he had purchased a pig at market, arrived home only to find a cat in his bag, the expression letting the cat out of the bag was borne. Both phrases come from the same context, with one attempting to buy a pig, but finding a poor substitution after the fact.

When metal pins were first invented around the 14th century, they were quite costly and scarce. As a matter of fact, so precious were they, that a law was decreed allowing women to purchase these pins only on January 1st and 2nd of each year. For this purpose, men were known to give their wives money to pur-

Pin Money

chase their yearly supply of pins. But when pins were no longer a monopoly and more readily come by, *pin money* became known as that money set aside for a woman to buy whatever niceties she might like from the allowance given her by her husband.

We use the word *powwow* today to connote a meeting at which there is much talk, most often in political context. The word, as you might imagine, comes from the native American Indian and does describe the

public feasts, dances and gatherings of certain tribes. It is generally used in political talk to signify any uproarious meeting at which there is more noise than deliberation; yet, while we use the term loosely today to describe such, we must keep in mind that the original *powwows* were noisy because they took place after success in war or in hunting.

Those unprofessional M.D.'s we might fondly refer to as "quacks" were originally known as quacksalvers. By definition and reputation, these were the cure-all medicine peddlers of the early 16th century, that quacked out the benefits of their salves and tonics as they traveled from town to town. These traveling medicine men were  more often known for their entertainment styles than their healing powers, but since they were generally recognized as quacksalvers, they became known as *quacks* for short.

That state of perplexity or doubt that we would call "being in a *quandary*" is believed to have originated some four centuries ago. An earlier phrase coined by the French,

"Qu'en dirai-je?" is about the best explanation etymologists have come up with for this perplexing word. By translation, "Qu'en dairai-je?" was interpreted, "What shall I make of it?" And as that question is precisely what a person in a *quandary* would ask, it is believed that it is the basis of our word *quandary* today.

As American as apple pie is the *quarter horse*, yet, contrary to popular belief, the breed was not named for its lineage or size. Rather the *quarter horse* was so named because of its ability to run high speeds in quarter-mile races. First named in 1834, the *quarter horse* is re-

cognized as a breed unto itself, somewhat smaller than thoroughbred racehorses, and characterized by great endurance and high speed in short distances. The earliest quarter horses were also known as quarter nags.

This phrase, used to connote strange or different, dates back to the late-1600s when Oliver Cromwell's son, Richard, attempted to rule England as Protector, after the reign of his father. While the word "queer" in this

context, had nothing to do with sexual preference, Queen Dick, as he was called, WAS known for his effeminate ways. Historically, "queer" wasn't associated with homosexuality until the 1920s, so it is assumed its reference here simply meant strange. Yet, as history has it, Dick's hatband, or crown, WAS considered strange upon the head of such a weak ruler.

Go to buy a ticket in America and you "line up," but do the same thing in Great Britain and you *queue up*. This English word that represents a line of people (or cars or things) was created from the French word "queue," which meant "little tail," or "pigtail." As a queue tends to curl around as a little tail would do, so goes the

meaning of the word. In any event, both English and French references date back to the original Latin word, "cauda," also meaning tail.

From Latin, *quid pro quo* specifically means, "something for something," and that same "something" (*quid*), is the root word for Britain's pound sterling, used today.

Quid
Pro Quo

Originally, the phrase *quid pro quo* meant something, (usually money) that was given in exchange for something else. While its first reference is unknown, Shakespeare used a similar expression in his "Henry VI" when he wrote "I cry you mercy, 'tis but Quid for Quo."

The word we might use to describe the purest and most concentrated form of a thing, was in the beginning, designed to be a scientific explanation for things unseen. As medieval alchemists sought to find a fifth element to add to the existing earth, air, fire and water, *quinta essentia*, or a "fifth essence," was theorized, and believed

Quint-essence

to be a form of ether. Studied as the substance of all heavenly bodies, this *quintessence* came to mean the most essential part or the primary material of any material or idea.

The torture treatment known as the rack was introduced into the Tower of London in the mid-1400s. Its name was derived from the German word "recken," which meant "to

To Rack One's Brain

stretch or draw out," and the punishment itself, did just that. While this cruel and unusual torture treat-

ment was banned in England less than 200 years later, the image of one racking or stretching his brain has remained a common figure of speech within the English language ever since.

That fun-loving music that's come to be known as *ragtime* is precisely what its name implies. At a time when most music was very regimented and very precise in rhythm (as were waltzes and traditional ballads), *ragtime* music had no strict standard, and so was named literally for

its *ragged* time. Known as the precursor of jazz, *ragtime* music, with its syncopated melody and its accented accompaniment, became most popular around the turn of the century.

Perhaps we all know that reimbursing has to do with paying someone back, or making restoration by way of payment for an equivalent sum of money, but the part you might NOT have known is just how literal the

translation is. Derived from three Latin words, "re" meant "back," "im" meant "in" and "bursa" was the Latin word for "purse." So as we interpreted it, first from the Latin, and then from the French, *reimburse* meant to literally put the money back in another's purse. (If only they were all this easy!)

A *roughshod* horse was one whose shoes had nails protruding through. The concept was originally designed for horses on the battlefield, and the goal was to keep the animal from slipping. However, once on the battlefield, it was soon determined that *rough-shod* horses not only held a better grip, but they were also able to  do damage to any enemy that might have fallen in the fight. (Imagine the gory scene of one trampled by a *roughshod* horse! That same image will give you the meaning of "treating someone brutally," that we associate with the word *roughshod* today.)

With the advent of gold and silver coins, came the production of counterfeit money as well, and at one point in time, the only sure way to tell if a coin were solid was to drop the coin and listen for the tone it produced.

It was said that a solid, true coin would *ring true*, while a counterfeit, (one filled with an alloy of nickel or copper) would sound flat. The test was known as *ringing a coin*, and it was later determined to be less than reliable. In any event, the practice led to the phrase, "*rings true*," in connoting something that proves to be accurate.

When a person's name earns a word all its own, then it stands to reason that this was one impressive person! Such is true of Caesar Ritz, the Swiss restaurateur and hotel magnate, who built the famous Ritz Hotel in Paris in 1898. Known for his strict standards of excellence, Ritz earned the reputation of being the greatest  hotelier in all of the Western World. Once Ritz Hotels were established in London, New York and a handful of other prestigious cities, having something, "like the Ritz," or *Ritzy* became the standard description for anything extravagant and lavish.

Granted, the cocky way of a barnyard rooster certainly would fit the description of one who *rules the roost*, but the phrase is believed to reference something entirely different. In its original form, *rule the roost*

Rule the
Roost

was first recorded, *rule the roast!* It came from Old England and was made in reference to the master of the house who sat at the head of the table and served his guests. As *ruler of the roast*, that lord and master was responsible for both family and servants, and was indeed the authoritative figure for the household.

The *scapegoat,* or one that takes the blame for another, is Biblical in origin. The first recorded reference to which is found in Leviticus 26:10 where we are told that Aaron (brother of Moses) was instructed to bring two goats to the door of the tabernacle. As scripture has it, "...Aaron shall cast lots upon the two goats; one

lot for the Lord, and the other lot for the *scapegoat.*" The result was that the *scapegoat* was to be presented as a live offering unto the Lord, and thus, allowed to go free. Some believe the word to be a contraction of "escape goat."

To go *scot free* means to get off without paying. The word scot, from the Anglo-Saxon word "sceot," was a tax or a fine. The most common use of the word dates back to Old

England where a "scot and lot" was a levy placed on all subjects according to their ability to pay. Now technically speaking, the first scot was a form of income tax. But today, *scot free* simply means getting off the hook without paying, be it tax or otherwise.

It is from the Islamic faith that we derive the phrase *seventh heaven*. For it is the belief of the Muhammadans that there are seven levels of heaven, each progressively better than the previous one, each requiring a purer life to attain. According to Mohammed, the *seventh heaven* is

formed of "...divine light beyond the power of the tongue to describe." It is in this *seventh heaven* that pure bliss is found, as it is believed this is where God himself resides with his angels.

We usually refer to the "WHOLE *shebang*" when using this word, and by inference, we mean an entire lot or establishment. The word itself is believed to have come from the Irish word "shebeen," which was an

unlicensed, or illegal drinking establishment of old. As this particular type of speakeasy was known for its brawls and fights, it was said that a drunken Irishman could often be heard challenging "*the whole shebeen*," and thus, the meaning for the word today.

While we use the word *shoddy* today to mean a product that is inferior in quality, *shoddy* was originally a technical term used to describe a by-product that came from manufacturing wool. Some years ago, *shoddy* referred to the fluff part of weaving cloth that was thrown off in the spinning. While this fluff was

still used to make new wool, it was short-stapled, which meant the clothes made from it did not last as long. As that fabric was inferior to the long-stapled or combing wools, it became known as *shoddy*, and hence our reference today.

It was Etienne de Silhouette, the Comptroller General of France in 1759, for whom these black on white pictures were named. History tells us that under Silhouette's administration, businesses were ordered, in the name of savings, to

do away with all unnecessary details. By the same rule, even paintings were reduced to mere outlines. As a result, black on white portraits became popular, and were called *silhouettes* in honor of the financier whose economic plan had suggested them.

Yes, there IS an actual devise called a *slapstick*, and as you might imagine, it did originate with the vaudeville comedian. The *slapstick* was made of two flat pieces of wood, fastened at one end. When used by an

actor to hit another person, the *slapstick* was known to make an unusually loud noise, and thus, it produced

laughter when used in the vaudevillian's act. Back then, the *slapstick* was an actual prop. Today we use the word to sum up the horseplay and comedy that so often accompanied such sticks.

Earlier we referred to a *speakeasy* when describing *the whole shebang*. Well, the Irish are to thank for this word too, as it had to do with their prohibition laws of long ago. Contrary to such laws, one was not allowed

to raise his voice riotously or start a brawl in any establishment where liquor was sold. To do so might call to the attention of the police, the existence of the illegal establishment. The result was that patrons of such were to *speak easy*, both in the joint, as well as about it! Today *speakeasies* are simply known as places where illegal alcohol is sold!

The history has it, the first turkey talk went something like this: After a day of hunting, a white man and an Indian were dividing their spoils of three crows and two wild turkeys. The white man gave the Indian the first bird, a crow, as he took for himself a turkey. Next he gave the Indian another crow, and took for himself the second

Talking Turkey

turkey. Upon giving the Indian the third crow, the Indian objected, and the white man pointed out that the Indian was given three birds to his two, to which the Indian replied, "We stop talk birds, we now talk turkey."

Being *on tenterhooks* brings up feelings of anxiety, suspense and discomfort and by definition, the term literally is a stretch. *Tenter* we take from the Latin word "tendere," which means to stretch, which is precisely

what was done on *tenterhooks*. Cloth, once it was woven, used to be stretched or *tenterhooked* on hooks passed through the selvages. The literal translation gave way to the figurative image of one being stretched to the point of discomfort, when it was first used by Sir Walter Scott in his novel "Redgauntlet."

No, this dam had nothing to do with profanity, rather it had to do with something of very little value. A *tinker's dam* was a dam made of dough or clay that was used to confine the molten solder of a pot or pan in repair. As its purpose was solely to keep the solder from spreading where it was not needed, once it had 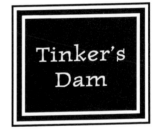 served its usefulness, the *tinker's dam* was discarded. As a result of this frequently used and virtually worthless solution, a *tinker's dam* has become almost universally synonymous with something worth nothing.

The origin of *true blue* as it pertains to one totally honest, faithful and dependable has more than one history. The first, they say, had to do with the fast dyeing qualities of the English color, "coventry blue." Now whether

it was actually coventry blue or not, it is noted that blue was adopted as the official color of the Pro-Parliament Scottish Presbyterian Party in 17th century England. And as this was chosen to be a direct contradistinction to the royal red of the Royalist Party, those said to be *true blue*, were considered to be among the loyalists and the faithful.

As we know from, "Two bits, four bits, six bits . . . a dollar," a couple of bits must be worth about a quarter. Originally, our dollar was based on the Spanish dollar, which could easily be divided into eight parts (hence, "pieces of eight!"). In the West Indies where Spanish money was widely used, paper dollars

were at one time, cut up into eight parts, with each being referred to as a "bit." As one bit was equal to 12 and a half cents, *two bits* was the equivalent of a quarter today... obviously a sum not worth very much; thus, our reference to something pretty cheap!

Think of a *tycoon* and you're probably envisioning one of great wealth and power. Truth is, the Japanese gave us the word; it comes from "tai," meaning "great," and "kun," which means "prince." The interesting part is

that the Japanese did not use the word among themselves, but rather used it only when speaking to foreigners in attempts to impress them with their own importance. It was Commodore Perry who brought the word back from Japan in the mid-1850s. We've been using it ever since to describe our own shoguns.

True, we use the phrase as though it means humble, but the original word was *umble*. *Umbles* (in case you didn't know), are the entrails of deer. Long ago, when hunters would prepare the venison from a hunt, the insides or entrails were saved and prepared in a pie for the servants to eat. As these servants obviously humbled

themselves to eat the less desirable portions, eating *umble pie* became the pun, and stood as a symbol for one who subordinates himself to another.

Historically, the original *Uncle Sam* was one, Samuel Wilson, co-owner of a slaughterhouse in Troy, New York, that was responsible for selling pork and beef to the U.S. army during the War of 1812. The meat

sold to the U.S. government by Sam and his uncle, Elbert Anderson, was stamped "E.A.-U.S." (for "Elbert Anderson - United States"). Story has it that a soldier once asked what the initials stood for and was told, "Elbert Anderson's Uncle Sam," after which the *Uncle Sam* part soon spread as the national nickname for the U. S. government.

This one has several variations, including, *Up Salt Creek*, or *Up a Creek Without a Paddle*. There's even the euphemism that we won't go into here. In any event, *Up a Creek* refers to being in a bad predicament, and the expression dates back some 100 years ago. Originally, it WAS Salt Creek that one was up, when he was in a tight

spot. The reference is to a creek leading through salt marshes or stagnant waters, where one would be stuck without an oar. The phrase was popularized in an 1884 political campaign song entitled "Blaine Up Salt Creek."

Some believe the idiom *upper hand* has to do with the age old game wherein two individuals place hand over hand along a stick or bat, until one reaches the top. Obviously, according to the rules of this

Upper Hand

common game, the *upper hand* is the winner. However, historically, the phrase pre-dates the invention of this game by some 200 years. It is believed that *upper hand*, used to connote authority or seniority, came from the now obsolete *over hand*, which was the term used to mean one having mastery or control over another.

Why would *upstage* refer to the rear of the stage rather than the part UP front? Well, it has to do with staging of old, when the actual back part of the stage was elevated. The *upstage* was designed so that actors on the back of the stage stood taller than the those toward the front, thus placing all players in full view for the sake

of the audience. Yet as *upstaged* actors stood literally taller than the rest, the reference to one upstaging another, soon came to mean one taking an elevated position for himself whether he deserved it or not!

A couple of theories exist on the origin of this phrase...The first being that *snuff* is really a derivative of *sniff*, and as smell is the most sensitive of all our senses, being *up to sniff* meant all senses were intact, (i.e. One is feeling fine!). The second theory has to do with tobacco. As snuff has long been the cheapest form of the product, and more easily come by than cigars or cigarettes, one not *up to snuff* was one who was flat broke indeed! Whether is broke physically or mentally, *up to snuff* still has to do with being up to a certain standard of well being.

Up To
Snuff

Vandals today destroy, damage and deface property, and the original Vandals did much the same. The first Vandals, a tribe of some 80,000 living around 450 A.D., may best be remembered for sacking Rome, and later persecuting early Christians. As the Vandals were responsible for destroying many valuable cultural ob-

jects along the way, the word *vandalism* now signifies wanton destruction, especially as it pertains to fine art. Technically the word *vandal* means "wanderer," as the tribe was known for its wandering conquests throughout France, Spain and Africa.

That wonderful form of stage entertainment known as *Vaudeville* was named for the place of its origin, *Vau de Vire*, which is located in the northwest part of France. *Vire* was both a river and a town in Normandy, that became famous for its unique form of theatrics, as well as for its

songs and short plays. Translated to mean "Valley of the Vire," *Vaudeville* soon became synonymous with the pantomimes, dancing, skits and songs associated therewith.

Today's word describing a jury's decision at the end of a trial is one that dates back to the Middle Ages. With the introduction of the jury, it was superstitiously believed that 12 men in a group would hold some mystical power in drawing a truthful conclusion. (The number 12 was considered holy both in reference to the 12  tribes of Israel and Jesus's 12 apostles.) It was the French who gave this body of 12 the name of "vrai" ("true") and "dit" ("said"). Even in homicide cases today, a *verdict* cannot be obtained until all 12 on the jury reach an agreement.

Once thought to be associated with witch-craft, ventriloquism has to do with that unique talent of producing a voice that appears to be coming from some place other than the speaker's mouth. Originally, that

sound was thought to be coming from the stomach, hence, the name *ventriloquist*. From the Latin, "ventri" meaning "belly," and "loqui" meaning "to speak," the first ventriloquists were said to be those who "spoke from their bellies." Later, the art was improved to the point that the sound seemed to be coming from such places as a dummy or a corner of a room!

Distilled from a mash of rye, barley or even potatoes, *vodka* was invented by the Russians and named by them as well. While its name was derived from the Russian word "voda," meaning "water," *vodka* was not originally named such because of its water-like appearance. Rather it was so named because at the time of its invention, it

was believed that the spirits of *vodka* were as essential to life as water, itself! Incidentally, "whiskey" comes from a word meaning water as well, ("aquivit," in Scandinavian) and for the same reason!

The literal and figurative symbol that we use to represent the financial interests of the U.S. economy was originally named for a wall once situated there. Located in downtown Manhattan, *Wall Street* derived its name

from an actual wall that extended the entire length of the street when the Dutch first settled in this country. Since the early 19th century, *Wall Street* has been known for the financial institutions located along the wall, and to this day, we fondly remember the street by way of the wall that once stood in its place.

Referring to one who is naive, immature... anything less than wise by the ways of the world, and you're talking *wet behind the ears*. As the image might suggest, this wetness has to do with the likes of a newborn, be it a hu-man, a calf, a colt, etc. As you might imagine, the last place to dry on a newborn is that small place behind the ears;

Wet Behind the Ears

thus, the image connotes the innocence of one just starting to make his way in the world, but who has barely left the safety of his first surroundings.

It was King Edward VI, the feeble son of England's Henry VIII, for whom we had the first *whipping boy*. Because King Edward VI WAS so sickly in his youth, it was decided that another should take his punishments for him. Barnaby Patrick was the unfortunate lad who was selected to take whippings on behalf of the

King. While England used the *whipping boy* idea for centuries, Fitzpatrick is the one first credited with the job! Today we use *whipping boy* to connote anyone punished for the mistakes of another, especially when a worker takes the heat for a superior.

The phrases we now use to describe differences in work force classes, date back to the early-1920s. The *white-collars* were those who performed non-manual labor, (or duties not requiring work clothes) and included office workers and those who had not joined unions. *Blue collars* referred to those who worked with their

hands, most often for an hourly wage, most often in unions. Interestingly enough, the counterparts to white-collars and blue-collars in England are black-coats and hard-hats, respectively; again, so named for the types of jobs the worker performed.

To send someone on a *wild goose chase* means to waste time pursuing a thing that perhaps, didn't merit pursuing in the first place. According to sources, the problems associated with *wild goose chases* are two-fold. First, the wild goose is a difficult bird to catch, and second, even if caught, there's not much you can do

with a wild goose, once you catch it! Therefore, to send a person on a *wild goose chase* means you've put him in pursuit of something not very practical, and at best, it's not worth the energy expended if caught.

Most know *sowing wild oats* has to do with giving up one's youthful, wild and often immature ways, but Scandinavian folklore gives a fuller meaning. According to legend, thick fogs and vapors would rise from the earth just before the land would blossom into vegetation. In Denmark, they referred to these vapors as

(Sowing One's) Wild Oats

"Lokkens havre," which translated into "Loki's wild oats!" As the god of strife and evil in Norse mythology, Loki was believed to transform himself into one last mystical mist before settling down to a season of productive harvests.

Granted, most folks know that the origin of *win, place or show* dates back to the earliest racetracks. But most may not know that the phrase was so named because of the way in which the finishes were announced. As small

boards were used to record the names of the winners of each horse race, and as these boards were SO small that only the first two could be "placed" on the board, the titles "win" and "place" were soon coined. Shortly after, a second board was used to "show" the third winner, and *win, place or show* became synonymous with first, second and third!

The original "X" used to designate a kiss dates back to medieval times, and believe it or not, it was a legal custom! In attempts to show good faith, the "X" (symbol for St. Andrew), was placed after each signature on papers of importance. To further reinforce the pledge made in the documents, the signee was required to kiss the "X" as a

guarantee of his or her obligation. Over time, the association with the legal profession has been long forgotten, but the "X" we still remember as the sign for a kiss!

While some consider it disrespectful to substitute an "X" for the Christ part of Christmas, others know that the letter "X" was in fact, the symbol used long ago for

Xmas

Christ. "X" represents the Greek letter "chi," which is the initial letter of the Greek word for Christ. And according to first century history, the early Greek Christians used the letter "X" to stand for Christ, much as they used the fish with the "X" in the tail to represent Jesus.

From the Greek words "xylo," meaning "wooden," and "phone," meaning "sound," the first *xylophone* was an invention of the native African, and it was used for chasing away evil spirits. Later the wooden sounds became a common form of entertainment, and later yet, the idea of adding tubular resonators under the bars

to increase the sound, gave birth to the marimba. From the marimba, a keyboard was later added, giving us the celesta, (the French word for "heavenly").

In case you didn't know, a *Yankee Dime* is a kiss, and the origin of such has to do with certain behaviors and characteristics common to one portion of the population, though not necessarily another. Folklore has

it that the "Yankees" of this new country were so thrifty, that they would often attempt to pay for something with a kiss rather than a coin! A similar (though not as common) colloquialism was the *Quaker fip* (which was a 5 cent piece), used as the reverse of the *Yankee dime*!

Perhaps you think of *yahoos* as bumpkins or hicks, but their true identity is really much worse. The Yahoos, as they were first described, were just a notch above barbaric beasts. Yahoos came from Jonathan Swift's famous "Gulliver's Travels." It was in his fourth and last voyage that Gulliver traveled to the land of the ed-

ucated horse, the Houyhnhnms, who held as slaves, the nasty, human animals they called "Yahoos." According to Swift's depiction, the Yahoos were the worst that could be found in all mankind, and so goes the meaning we associate with it today.

To spin a *yarn*, as it refers to telling a tale, is originally naval talk that dates back to the early 19th century. It is believed that the *yarn* here has to do with the *yarn* lofts of old, wherein yarn was spun to supply the ships with rope. As the interweaving of the threads and the spinning of the twine took much time in the

(to spin a) Yarn

development, so too, was the case in the telling of a really good story. Add to that, the obvious pastime of gossip that most often accompanied the task of yarn-weaving, and you've *spun a good yarn*, while telling a really juicy tale!

By translation, *yule* is Norse for jolly, and such was the mood at Yuletime festivals of old. Originally a heathen holiday, later changed by Catholic priests into a Christian event, the celebration of *yule* kicked off the winter solstice. At the time of this shortest day of the year, a 12-day feast was held, marked by the burning

of the lighted *yule* log, and the singing of carols. Today we have the 12 Days of Christmas as a salute to the feast of the *Yule*, and we sing Yuletide carols in celebration!

Leave it to the French to name the peel of a lemon or orange for the kick it added to food and drink! Dating back to the 17th century, the word *zest* was derived from the Latin

word "scistus," meaning "cut." By taking this cut of citrus, and adding it to everything from basic water to fine cuisine, the French created both a flavorful (*zesty*) addition for their sense of taste, and a creative new word for their colorful vocabulary!

Yes, those pointed little remarks made to "zing" another, actually had an origin! The namesake is one, John Peter Zenger, who, in 1735 served time for his outspoken political barbs made in the New York Weekly Journal. As William Cosby, Colonial Governor of New York at the time, was the primary recipient of these remarks, (and as Cosby was less than happy about the bad press), Zenger was jailed for 8 months without a trial, for seditious libel. Though later acquitted by a jury, Zenger is remembered today for the barbing technique he made famous!

(My thanks to John Seigenthaler, Chairman of the Freedom Forum First Amendment Foundation, for the story behind this one!)

In Closing...

As my best "I Didn't Know That's" came to me from historians and storytellers recalling phrase origins they were told, I welcome the stories *you've* heard.

Have something to contribute?

Send your "I Didn't Know That's" to:

"I Didn't Know That"
P.O. Box 150263
Nashville, TN 37215

If your word or phrase adds something new to our research, and is selected for use in a future volume of "I Didn't Know That," I'll gladly send you your very own autographed copy of your story in print!

Thanks for your support!

Karlen Evins